D0875950

SHARON STONE

SHARON STONE

With an essay by Tom Kummer

Plexus, London

A British Library Catalogue record for this book is available
from the British Library.

Translated from the German by Roger W. Benner.
Cover design by John Mitchell
Separations: NovaConcept, Berlin
Typesetting: Typograph, Munich
Printing and binding: EBS, Verona

SHARON STONE

Oscar night 1997. The clear sky above Los Angeles glistened brightly as if something gigantic were taking place — a riot or an inferno. Outside the entrance to Mortons Restaurant Hollywood seethed. Sharon Stone stepped from her Rolls-Royce into a waiting throng of cameras and microphones. The photographers' flashes resembled an artillery attack. Extras and bodyguards pushed and shoved a willing Sharon Stone into the restaurant, where Hollywood's foremost celebrities had already gathered for the *Vanity Fair* Oscar party. She waved as she ran the gauntlet, but no one waved back. She gave a friendly smile, but no one else smiled. She appeared both exhausted and tender — as tender as one can look in black leather pants. Her blue eyes were alight with innuendo. Sharon Stone strode silently past the agents and the lackeys of studio bosses who had once seriously claimed she possessed "the biggest balls in Hollywood", and who now were waiting lecherously to see those balls slowly fried. She strode past women who envied her for her greatest strengths: the art of seduction and control. No one in Hollywood could imagine that this woman no longer wanted the dirty job of sex goddess. She leaned against the bar like a drunken sailor and called for a glass of water while a hostess from *Vanity Fair* served Moët and caviar. The star turned unexpectedly in the direction where she suspected cameras and microphones to be and spoke the following words with a strangely official intonation: "I have done everything one has to do in this business. I put my money down, and I won. And now I want everything that goes with it — all the privileges and all the respect — because I've earned it."

But she spoke to an empty room. The cameras and microphones hadn't followed her. Only five people were listening: her agent Sherry Lansing, Todd McCarthy from *Variety*, two bodyguards, and myself. We stood mesmerized before the most fascinating woman that Hollywood had produced in the nineties, aware that the absence of the press showed that her career was in the doldrums and searched for signals that might perhaps herald a resurrection.

In January of 1996, Sharon Stone had signed a contract with Miramax, and she was hoping for new impetus for 1997 from the "Oscar specialists". She went to work on a screenplay based on the magical realism of her favourite authors Gabriel Garcia Marquez and Jorge Luis Borges. And then there were plans for the remake of the 1958 cult classic *Bell, Book, and Candle* in which she would play Kim Novak's role as the witch. That was all.

But one year earlier, Sharon Stone had been at the peak of her career in the Beverly Hills Hotel. She won the Golden Globe for her role in Martin Scorsese's film *Casino*, and she was on the verge of tears when she spoke into the microphone: "You really like me, at last." She was nominated for an Oscar, but she won a little respect, which Hollywood usually doesn't show a sex goddess.

"Do you know what the difference between the Bond girls and Sharon Stone is?" *Variety* reporter McCarthy asked me at the time.

I could imagine, but I didn't answer.

"James Bond wouldn't have lasted thirty seconds in bed with Sharon Stone."

McCarthy belonged to the group of Hollywood reporters who scoffed at Sharon Stone's acting ability yet, like millions of men, had been incessantly turned on by her, and therefore said things like: "Sharon Stone screws her men. Not the other way around."

It was exactly this fantasy that was the secret of Miss Stone's success.

Sharon Stone looked fantastic on that catastrophic Oscar night. But no one was interested. The previous year, she had appeared in two hapless films — *Les Diaboliques* and *Last Dance*. And she had followed a path that usually ends in embarrassment in Hollywood: she wanted to try her hand at more serious roles and prove herself as a serious actress. It was this new deliberation that made her so exciting at Mortons. She smiled, and her face seemed so refreshing. It was as if Ginger, the drug-addicted, alcoholic *femme fatale* in Martin Scorsese's *Casino*, had just been released from the Betty Ford Clinic. On this Oscar night, she seemed to feel far removed from the world's preoccupation with what was going on outside the entrance to Mortons.

Shortly before making her little-noticed departure, Sharon Stone told me that today nothing that happens between her and Hollywood's powerful men, nothing that they had to say to one another, could influence her life for more than a single second. For her, every relationship — whether business or personal — is nothing more than a briefly fulfilling, speedily consummated example of life's variety.

There is no harsher or truer way of describing the power struggles of Hollywood.

*

I met Sharon Stone for the first time in the summer of 1992 during an interview at the Beverly Hills Hotel over her most successful film to date, *Basic Instinct*. At the time, I thought her on-screen sex was little more than soft-pornographic folly — embarrassing, sad, false — produced for ageing travelling salesmen. I didn't yet know that Sharon Stone had much more to offer. That something became apparent in the real world, not on the screen.

Her partner in *Basic Instinct*, Michael Douglas, once said in an interview: "You see, it's like this with Sharon. Everyone wants to get inside her. But the real problem is how to get out once you've gotten inside her." At the Beverly Hills Hotel, I met a woman who knew the truth about her own feelings. She knew that her feelings had no ethical foundation and little consistency. I sensed the potential for terrible pain. I felt how her pulse quickened as if she wanted to divulge something. Her role in *Basic Instinct* had put her on a dangerous course, one that usually ends in hell. But Sharon Stone had a plan. She wanted to survive as a blonde sex goddess in Hollywood.

Back then at the hotel, Sharon Stone lit up a Hernandez cigarillo. She nervously paced her suite. Then she motioned me over to the window. She needed some light, she said. She pulled up her pants, dramatizing her movements as she did so. Then she said: "My face changes constantly. Sometimes I weigh 135 pounds, then I weigh 155 pounds. And I have all sizes imaginable in my closet. Now I've decided on a medium size and destroyed all the other clothes. And I fired my fitness trainer, as well. All this fuss about my figure doesn't bother me anymore. As a woman approaching 40, I want to concentrate on other things. Whoever wants me has to accept me as I am. If worse comes to worst, I'll just have to take Slim-Fast …"

"A weight reducer?" I asked and felt like an idiot.

"Exactly. Tastes like chocolate milk, but it doesn't have any side effects."

At the window, her beautiful high forehead was well-illuminated by the sun. She seemed as tempting as Kim Novak in *Vertigo*, whose innocence Alfred Hitchcock had so skillfully employed — as a pure object of seduction. People react to her with jealousy — and millions of American men still think of a dumb blonde when they see nudity on the screen. Sharon lets the envious and the sexists fall into the same trap, however, and there is no escape. She ran her middle finger over a glass of water. She said she had been tormented here in the darkness for the past four hours; that she hated interviews; that she was usually the one who tortured men, not the other way around. But what she didn't mention is that she usually plays a comedienne, not a diabolical dominatrix. Unfortunately, Hollywood hasn't realized that yet. Sharon Stone would be a fantastic comedienne, but what man wants a sex goddess to make him laugh?

She shot me a quick glance and then turned her gaze almost ashamedly towards the brightly illuminated Persian rug. Then she claimed in all seriousness that the only way of coping with altruism was, in her opinion, extreme poverty or great wealth. It was an absurd sociological explanation, smacking of paranoia, an uneasy conscience, and slight insanity, such as only women in Hollywood can deliver. She knew exactly which alternative she preferred. At such moments, Sharon Stone seems far removed from the wonderland of male dreams: she is simply a woman with blonde hair. Suddenly, she broke the silence. "I'm not the woman in *Basic Instinct*, but hardly anyone believes that. I can't understand why they won't free me from this burden. I portray a kind of sexuality that is completely foreign to me. I'm no sex-neurotic who constantly rolls around in silk sheets. I'm more a person who sits alone at home in my flannel pajamas, reads a screenplay, and says: 'This person wouldn't do that or that in the movie.' I am a total realist, if you know what I mean."

No, I had no way of knowing that.

Everything really began in 1990 with the futuristic film *Total Recall* — the first film for which Sharon received good reviews that did not merely praise her sexual aura. The role of "Robo-chick" Barbie in Paul Verhoeven's futuristic thriller was the spark that set off her career. She was finally able to prove that her potential far exceeded dumb blonde roles, she was dazzling in a couple of fantastic kung-fu scenes, for example. That was all, but it was enough to fire the imaginations of the producers. The result was *Basic Instinct* — a sweeping breakthrough that introduced one of the most powerful female images of the nineties.

Until the late eighties, Sharon had only appeared in films that were produced expressly for the video market. She was over thirty and still at the bottom of the casting list; but then she landed the role of the blonde, bisexual, man-eating Catherine Tramell. Director Verhoeven handed her an ice pick, and she left her underwear in the dressing room. It was a role that had been prudely declined by all of Hollywood's female stars, even the 12-million-dollar woman Demi Moore, who usually wasn't so choosy.

The role in *Basic Instinct* strongly resembled a "Madonna *magna cum laude*" who flashed her breasts and pubic hair and thus led men to their doom. This was also the attitude she adopted during my interview at the Beverly Hills Hotel: "It's great to be famous because now I can torture powerful men."

Of course, such utterances were more a matter of fun and clever Hollywood tactics than stupidity. But few realized that. The critics looked upon Sharon Stone as a passing craze, as just another blonde who would disappear, naked and ravaged, into the dark pits of Hollywood. But things took a different turn.

In *Basic Instinct*, Sharon revives the classic *what you see is what you get* sex-bomb image of Mae West, Marlene Dietrich, and

Marilyn Monroe. To date, the film has grossed over $300 million, including video sales. Leading man Michael Douglas raked in $15 million while Miss Stone had to make do with $400,000. But she hasn't since dropped below the $3 million mark. Much more important, however, was the image that she created for herself in *Basic Instinct*. She transformed sex in the cinema from a secret into a spectacle, without having to take off her clothes; and that enabled her to reach a position of power such as no Hollywood actress had ever achieved in such a short time and which can only be compared with Madonna's sway in the pop-music business. At the Beverly Hills Hotel, Sharon sipped dreamily from her champagne glass and nonchalantly rolled her cigarillo in the corner of her mouth, looking like some kind of James Dean on heroin. It wasn't until then that I noticed her eyes looked as if she had been crying.

"You know, what really depresses me is that as far as my role in *Basic Instinct* is concerned, the public is much more concerned about whether I'm a lesbian than whether I'm a serial killer. I have to ask myself: people, what are your priorities?"

She laughed. She pressed her lips together and made a little smacking noise. She looked away in order to collect her thoughts. It was one of those moments men dread.

She has had no relationship to date that has lasted more than three years. She doesn't care. During fifteen years of Hollywood, she has learned to capitalize mercilessly on her self-confidence despite constant setbacks and overwhelming sexism. It cost her a lot of energy — blondes are a dime a dozen in Hollywood — but it was her only chance. For years she was shown no respect. A woman who undresses one time in front of Hollywood's cameras is an outcast for life.

Today, it is precisely her power of endurance that strikes fear into the hearts of Hollywood's macho producers. She is to the point, quick, and clever. Sometimes she seems positively crazy. On the other hand, she can turn to ice when the situation demands it; but her strongest weapon is self-control.

"I'm not going to take any more crap. I grind my teeth and tell those guys to go to hell. People say I have the biggest balls in Hollywood. And everyone is afraid of that. And as long as those people are afraid, I'll keep my job."

What a lot of people didn't know at the time of *Basic Instinct* was that the girl from Meadville, Pennsylvania — a town with two intersections and one stoplight — has one of the highest IQs ever registered in Crawford County: 154. (In Hollywood, only Gena Davis comes close with an IQ of 153.) Another thing that was never really noted in Hollywood, and which could have saved many powerful men a lot of aggravation, was the fact that her father Joe was a simple store owner with socialist convictions and an avowed feminist to boot. His own father died when he was young, and he was raised by a number of women. During a telephone interview, he once said: "I like to see women like my daughter Sharon get a fair chance in this world. They didn't get one long enough."

*

In July of 1995, I was sitting beside Sharon Stone in a black Jeep Wrangler. The subject was *Casino* — the final revelation; the grandiose conclusion of a Hollywood blonde's transformation.

"I am happy. My god, I am really happy!" She screamed the words towards the windshield as we headed west down Mulholland Drive. We were meeting for an interview, but Miss Stone had had enough of dark hotel rooms. So we talked in the jeep.

Sharon had just stolen the show from all the Italo-America film greats — among them Robert De Niro — in Martin Scorsese's gangster opus. *Casino* proved once again that she is the only female filmstar in Hollywood who knows what a true movie star owes her fans.

On the screen she proved that women can play in a veritable state of rapture when they link up with the right men — like Martin Scorsese and Robert De Niro, for example. Concerning her experiences with them, she said: "At first, it was like a hallucination. Bobby and Marty either demote you to an extra, or you play their game — it all depends on yourself. They dominate you. But the dominance of those men unleashes something unbelievably positive in a woman. And that is something you rarely come across. Until then, I had only experienced male dominance as an extreme hindrance. De Niro and Scorsese are among the few men from whom women can learn something. The filming of *Casino* was one of the most important events in my life until now. I had to stick it out; I cried a lot. Almost like in real life."

Some of the scenes in *Casino* must have certainly reminded Sharon Stone of her own life. In the role of call girl and cardsharp Ginger McKenna, she turns the head of casino boss/Mafioso

Robert De Niro, alias Sam "Ace" Rothstein. There is only one problem: although Ginger may cast lascivious glances across the gambling table, she isn't in love with Ace, but he wants to turn her into a good wife. Driven by pride and jealousy, like a modern-day Othello, Ace finally loses the woman and his casino.

"Of course I know this scene from my own life. A man, who is always somewhat of a bastard, usually realizes at a certain point in his life that he wants to be a good person. With a wife and a child and so on. He doesn't want to lose his power, of course, but he also wants to be a good husband. His good intentions alone convince him that he is right in forcing his wife to take the same path. And that is the great dilemma for many men: just because they provide everything, they believe they can make the rules and force their women to love them. No way, José, is all I have to say to that. I had a relationship like that once. The guy was a country singer. I could still slap myself for wasting valuable time with that guy."

Sharon Stone was referring to country singer Dwight Yoakam, but she didn't mention his name.

"Aren't problems with relationships inevitable for a sex symbol who is earning over 10 million dollars per film?"

"I want a partner who really loves me. That's all. But that is impossible for me, so to speak. My life has changed entirely since *Basic Instinct*. The movie-star machine is crushing me. Who wants to enter into a real relationship with me? I need a body-guard; strange men break into my house; I get thousands of letters every day, half of them written by psychopaths. But the worst part of it all is that every guy, nice as he may be, wants to have sex with me immediately. Although most of them don't really want to sleep with me; they just want other people to believe they slept with me."

"And what do you do about that?"

"Work and dominate. I go out alone; I don't need an escort or the drama of a wild relationship. But no one should think that I am trying to attain a fulfilled life and power by force and by putting on masculine airs. For me, that is misunderstood feminism. It's just that no one can scare me anymore. And I don't panic, anyway. I am much more scared of myself. Sometimes my character is like a really bad neighbourhood in Los Angeles, and my reason tells me I shouldn't go there alone."

Sharon Stone gazed out over the infinite cityscape of Los Angeles. She wanted to show me something out there, but apparently she had forgotten what it was. I noticed a tiny scar on her throat. A little later she told me that she had almost been strangled by a pair of reins during the filming of *The Quick and the Dead*, a western with Gene Hackman.

"I want to show you something," she said suddenly as she parked the car on Mulholland Drive. "Do you see how the electric lights sometimes shine in broad daylight in West Hollywood? For me, there is nothing more beautiful than this artificial freshness in the heart of the heat. Everything human is artificial here. That also fascinated me about Las Vegas. The desert bears all the elements of sacrifice: fire, light, and heat. The desert and Las Vegas are inseparable. You have to make a sacrificial offering to both … a man, for example … and consecrate him to the desert. If something of equal beauty has to disappear in it, why not a nice, attractive man?"

It took me a few minutes to recover from those words. Sharon Stone then went on to speak of the affinity between the austerity of the palace-like casinos and the austerity of the gambling at the tables, but I couldn't really follow what she was saying. My attention was suddenly caught up in her face, her bright eyes, her good-humoured smile that was more an expression of tribulations overcome than the happiness of a star at the pinnacle of her career. Was this really the same woman who tied up and beat her own daughter in a cocaine-induced frenzy in *Casino*? The same woman who rams her Cadillac into her husband's car in a fit of rage? The same woman whose menacing look puts an end to the dreams of all men?

Yes, the eyes were the same; it was the same woman who sells herself in Hollywood — with the radical ecstasy of a brutal Italian mobster. The real Ginger was one of Las Vegas' most respected call girls during the early seventies, and Sharon considered that title an honour.

"What fascinates me most about Ginger is her appreciation for excess. Where there is excess, there is also danger. Places where people live on the edge — and Las Vegas was the centre of human depravity at the time — bring forth great dramas."

Sharon Stone spoke these weighty words with the warmth of a slot machine. She had suddenly transformed herself from a sex symbol into a likeable monster. In order to reduce the tension, I said:

"Shall we take a little break?"

"Why," she asked. "Are you afraid of me?"

"No," I replied, "I just want to think for a minute."

"Typical. Take a break. But that's totally wrong. Come on, keep going!"

She had realized that we both have the same weird, discerning sense of humour, and we therefore treated each other with prudence and respect. But that "Come on, keep going!" was a clear warning not to play games with her.

"Is Hollywood in love with so-called 'hooker-chic' thanks to you?"

She didn't react at first. Then she shook her head as if the question affected her personally.

"I gave up a lot over the past years."

Sharon seemed to be answering a different question, one regarding her lovers. But I hadn't asked her about that.

"I quit trying to be complete in another person because that's impossible anyway. I also quit ignoring my own true feelings for the sake of others that I could perhaps have. During the eight relationships I've had in my life, I was so occupied with creating and then abandoning a complicated illusion of life that I lost track of my true objective."

"What was your objective, Miss Stone?"

"Simply to enjoy and to forget everything else."

"So you only use sex as a weapon on the screen, never in order to marshall power in real life?"

"Never! I prefer the duel-like art of seduction."

"Why?"

"Because love and sexuality are also metaphors for flinging

oneself into the abyss. Whoever wants to win, mustn't love. Seduce one another!"

I tried to retain my composure. Sharon had smiled, and she was starting to get to me. I mustn't lose control now. She was unbelievably attractive at this moment. Referring to the "hooker-chic" in which Hollywood had fallen in love, she said:

"The fantasies of both men and women converge in the role of the prostitute. Men see the embodiment of their most secret wishes. And for an actress, it is a tempting role because it is usually directed against the moral values of the mass audience, therefore permitting a certain degree of rebellion."

That was ludicrous, of course. Hollywood only accepts women who either have sex with extreme abandon or not at all. There is no middle ground. But at least I had freed myself from her stranglehold.

"Is there any future for a star like yourself?" Instead of answering, she leaned over the steering wheel and grinned at me: "Why do you ask that, young man?"

The long-term allure of Hollywood stars has seldom been shorter than it is today. During the forties and fifties, there were stars like Bette Davis, Joan Crawford, or Marilyn Monroe whom you could always count on. And Norma Desmond, the heroine in Billy Wilder's *Sunset Boulevard*, even said once that "stars are timeless beings".

"But Desmond doesn't live in today's Hollywood," Sharon screamed in disgust towards the windshield of her Jeep Wrangler.

"Today, stars come and go like Christmas trees. Why is that?"

She turned to face me and said: "Because careers are no longer decided by the studios; they are decided by agents who only want to please the audience's ever-changing tastes. I am in a position to make the audience, agents, and producers dance to my tune."

"You used an ice pick and spread your legs slightly on your way to power, is that correct? Do you have a future, Miss Stone?"

That was it. It's now or never, I thought to myself. Now she'll pull out the ice pick. But my time wasn't up yet. The game wasn't quite over.

"Dream about me," Sharon Stone said as our drive came to an end in front of her rose-coloured palazzo in Bel Air. A handful of paparazzi were hanging around outside the iron gate, hoping for pictures showing the sex goddess with her new lover. Sharon's greatest quality is not just assertiveness. She is a victor who knows that an evil spirit dwells at the core of all passionate emotions; she also knows that her powers of seduction were only exceeded by the illusion provided by the cinema: "Dream about me. That's what I was made for. I'm not good for much else," she said in closing. She said it to the paparazzi, to me, and to the millions of men and women out there. Judging by the way she said it, she seemed to view the world as an insignificant joke and her own comfortable life as some elitist club.

When I didn't get out at once, Sharon gave me a poke in the ribs, contorting her face and mouth as she did so. Rolling her cigarillo in the corner of her mouth, her expression seemed to demand from life a timeless, existential, and eternal youth. It seemed as though she was trying to give me a signal: as a sex goddess who no longer wants to be one, she feels obliged to mislead and to deviate from the truth. Be that as it may, she would prefer to speak only of the truth: to say that nothing is stronger than seduction, for example. And that we get ourselves into nothing but trouble when we try to explain sex symbols. Some things just can't be explained. They simply exist. And after a while they disappear without a trace, usually forever.

PLATES

Portrait from 1987, taken at the time the thriller *Action Jackson* was being filmed, a movie in which Sharon Stone played a minor supporting role. © Cinetext Bild- und Textarchiv GmbH, Frankfurt.

Basic Instinct: Scene with Michael Douglas. Photo: Carolco. © The Kobal Collection, London. **Publicity shot.** © dpa Bildarchiv, Munich.

Publicity shots for *Total Recall*, 1990: She played alongside Arnold Schwarzenegger in this science fiction film. © Cinetext Bild- und Textarchiv GmbH, Frankfurt.

Basic Instinct: Scene with Denis Arndt. Photo: Carolco. © Cinetext Bild- und Textarchiv GmbH, Frankfurt.

Sharon Stone in her most successful film, *Basic Instinct*, from 1992: Scene with Michael Douglas. © Alpha Photographic Press Agency Ltd., London. **Taken from the photo-series** for the film poster. © Studio X/Stills, Limours.

Stills from *Basic Instinct*. © Bildarchiv Engelmeier, Munich (left). © Alpha Photographic Press Agency Ltd., London (right).

Still from *Basic Instinct*. © Cinetext Bild- und Textarchiv GmbH, Frankfurt.

Sharon Stone with film partner William Baldwin in *Sliver*. © The Kobal Collection, London.

Sharon Stone at the opening of the International Film Festival in Cannes 1992, following her great success with *Basic Instinct*. Photo: Aslan. © Sipa Press, Paris.

1994: Richard Gere and Sharon Stone together in *Intersection*. She was hoping to create a new image for herself with a wife-and-mother role. © dpa Bildarchiv, Munich.

Still from *Sliver*, 1993. © Bildarchiv Engelmeier, Munich.

Publicity shots for *Intersection*. Photos: Takashi Seida. © Cinetext Bild- und Textarchiv GmbH, Frankfurt.

Fashion photo by Greg Gorman, 1992.
© Studio X/Liaison/Gamma, Limours.

Still with Rod Steiger (left) and James Woods in
The Specialist. Photo: Ron Phillips.
© The Kobal Collection, London.

Sharon Stone, photographed by Greg Gorman.
© Studio X/Liaison/Gamma, Limours.
Still from *The Specialist*, 1994.
© Pandis Media GmbH, Munich.

Taking a break from shooting by the swimming
pool, 1994. © Rex Features, London/Schweitzer
Bildarchiv, Munich (left).
© Action Press, Hamburg (right).

Sharon Stone and Sylvester Stallone in
The Specialist. Photo: Ron Phillips.
© The Kobal Collection, London.

During the shooting of *The Specialist* in Florida.
Photo: Philippe Brylak
© Studio X/Liaison/Gamma, Limours.
Making her appearance with a cigar at the
Comedy Hall of Fame. © Alpha Photographic
Press Agency Ltd., London.

Sharon Stone at the International Film Festival in Cannes, May 1995. Photos: Dave Hogan © Rex Features, London/Schweitzer Bildarchiv, Munich.

Still from *Casino*. Photo: Phillip Caruso. © Cinetext Bild- und Textarchiv GmbH, Frankfurt. Sharon Stone and Joe Pesci in *Casino*. Photos: Phillip Caruso. © The Kobal Collection, London.

Press frenzy in Cannes, 1995. Photo: Dave Hogan © Rex Features, London/Schweitzer Bildarchiv, Munich.
Portrait taken on February 25, 1996, in connection with a television interview in Paris. Photo: Nivière © Sipa Press, Paris.

Portraits by Greg Gorman, Los Angeles 1992 and 1994. © Studio X/Liaison/Gamma, Limours.

Sharon Stone with Robert De Niro in the film *Casino*, 1995. Martin Scorsese was the director. Photo: Phillip Caruso. © The Kobal Collection, London.

Scene from the Hollywood remake of Clouzot's *Les Diaboliques*, 1996. © Cinetext Bild- und Textarchiv GmbH, Frankfurt.

Sharon Stone in *Les Diaboliques*.
Photo: Morgan Creek. © The Kobal Collection,
London.

With Valentino at a party hosted by the American
ambassador at Maxim's, Paris, 1995. Photo: Bert-
rand Rindoff © Pandis Media GmbH, Munich.
Sharon Stone, who began her career as a model,
stepped onto the runway once more for Valentino,
Paris, October 1993. © Pandis Media GmbH,
Munich.

Isabelle Adjani co-starring with Sharon Stone
in *Les Diaboliques*. Photo: Jim Bridges.
© The Kobal Collection, London.

Highlight of the Valentino show: Sharon Stone
in a wedding-mini, and Valentino surrounded by
supermodels in red. © Studio X/Stills, Limours.

Portrait taken in 1995 during the filming of
Les Diaboliques. © Cinetext Bild- und Textarchiv
GmbH, Frankfurt.
Portrait by Takashi Seida, 1994. © Cinetext Bild-
und Textarchiv GmbH, Frankfurt.

Portrait by Peter Lindbergh for *Harper's Bazaar*,
New York, September 1995. © Peter Lindbergh.

BIOGRAPHICAL DATA

Sharon Stone was born on March 10, 1958, in the small town of Meadville, Pennsylvania. There, she spent the first seventeen years of her life with her three siblings, her mother Dorothy Stone, and her father Joseph Stone. Her father Joe worked as a toolmaker and later went into business for himself.

Owing to her extremely high IQ of 154, Sharon started school in 1963 at the age of five, beginning with the second grade. The "child wonder" didn't get along too well with children her age, however, and preferred dressing up and later appeared in plays. Her wish was to leave Meadville as soon as possible and to become an actress.

In 1975 she graduated from Saegertown High School. She later participated in a beauty contest for the title of Miss Crawford County, which she easily won, leading to an invitation to the Miss Pennsylvania contest in Philadelphia. There, it was suggested that she become a photo model. Sharon was ecstatic.

In December 1975 Sharon Stone travelled to New York in order to apply to the renowned Eileen Ford Model Agency. She was offered a contract and was soon one of the agency's top ten models. Trips to Europe and Japan were soon followed by the first cover photos for the American editions of *Vogue, Elle,* and *Stern.*

She got her first silent role in 1980 from Woody Allen; she appeared for a few seconds in his film *Stardust Memories* as the beautiful, desirable woman who can be seen through the window of a railway compartment during a dream sequence.

This was followed by several small roles in the ensuing years, the later ones primarily in adventure and action films.

In July, 1990, a series of black-and-white nudes appeared in the US edition of *Playboy*; the photos by Phillip Dixon kindled her image as Hollywood's new sex idol.

In 1993/94, a photo series in the French and German editions of *Vogue* followed as well as advertising photos for Italian tyre-maker Pirelli.

Her breakthrough in Hollywood finally came in 1992 with *Basic Instinct*.

She received millions for her subsequent film roles; but because she did not want to be classified forever with the image of a man-eating sex goddess, she tried her hand at more serious roles. The film industry and audiences didn't give her much of a chance, however, and none of her ensuing films to date has been able to duplicate her first enormous success.

FILMOGRAPHY

(does not include TV movies)

1980   *Stardust Memories*
Director: Woody Allen

1981   *Deadly Blessing*
Director: Wes Craven

1981   *Les Uns et les Autres*
Director: Claude Lelouch

1984   *Irreconcilable Differences*
Director: Charles Shyer

1985   *King Solomon's Mines*
Director: J. Lee Thompson

1986   *Allan Quatermain and the Lost City of Gold*
Directors: Gary Nelson; Newt Arnold

1986   *Police Academy 4: Citizens on Patrol*
Director: Jim Drake

1987   *Cold Steel*
Director: Dorothy Ann Puzo

1987   *Action Jackson*
Director: Craig R. Baxley

1987   *Above the Law*
Director: Andrew Davis

1989   *Personal Choice* a.k.a. *Beyond the Stars*
        Director: David Saperstein

1989   *Blood and Sand*
        Director: Javier Elorrieta

1990   *Total Recall*
        Director: Paul Verhoeven

1990   *Scissors*
        Director: Frank De Felitta

1991   *Where Sleeping Dogs Lie*
        Director: Charles Finch

1991   *Year of the Gun*
        Director: John Frankenheimer

1991   *He Said, She Said*
        Directors: Ken Kwapis; Marisa Silver

1992   *Diary of a Hitman*
        Director: Roy London

1992   *Basic Instinct*
        Director: Paul Verhoeven

1993   *Sliver*
        Director: Phillip Noyce

1993   *Last Action Hero*
        Director: John McTiernan

1994   *Intersection*
        Director: Mark Rydell

1994 *The Specialist*
   Director: Luis Llosa

1995 *The Quick and the Dead*
   Director: Sam Raimi

1995 *Casino*
   Director: Martin Scorsese

1996 *The Last Dance*
   Director: Bruce Beresford

1996 *Les Diaboliques*
   Director: Jeremiah Chechik

In the works:

1998 *The Mighty*
   Director: Peter Chelsom

1998 *Sphere*
   Director: Barry Levinson

1998 *Antz*
   Directors: Eric Darnell; Lawrence Guterman; Tim Johnson

1998 *Gloria*
   Director: Sidney Lumet